This Book is Published by

I0102916

Michael Almaraz CHT, NLP, RP

Michael@deeperstate.com

Deeper States Mind and Wellness

Los Angeles, Ca

Deeperstate.com

Author: Michael Almaraz

ISBN # 978-0-9916254-7-5

Cover Design – Empower Your Life Publishing

For those who like finding grammatical errors and typos, I have left a few for you to enjoy.

Abundantly You

A Guide to Creating Abundance and Balance in Your Life

By Michael Almaraz

TABLE OF CONTENTS

DEDICATION

With all the power and glory of the divine
energy of God and the universe,
I dedicate this to my brother:

Richard

I remember our times hunting and fishing along the Verde River. We grew up at an old power plant, of which my father was the caretaker. The old coal and steam plant, named TAPCO, was located about 35 miles outside Clarkdale, Arizona. We had a great but sometimes difficult life. At times, it was a very isolated and lonely way to grow up. I always knew that if I needed something or someone to tell me it was all going to be ok, He would be the one to do that.

The eight years between us seemed a lifetime, but we always understood each other perfectly.

Deep in my heart, I knew that I could always look up to and admire him, even though we argued and fought, as all siblings do. I found myself having to rewrite this dedication because, as I was finishing this book, he lost his battle with stage IV bone cancer. Richard looked as different from our siblings as he acted from them. His fiery red hair, white complexion and freckles made him a very special person and a strong, stubborn man. I remember that he told me to go out and live my life to its fullest, to just be myself.

I believe I have done just that, in every unconventional way possible – even to the point of becoming a known hypnotherapist and practitioner of Neuro-Linguistic Programming (NLP). We now know the outcome of this situation; he no longer needs to ask me about the plan for his treatment; my dear brother, now only you know God's plan.

Only you know the experience and outcome of death. I hope you always know that I loved you and thank you for teaching me to be a strong and motivated person, never giving up on my hopes or dreams.

With all my love:

Your brother,

Michael

We had joy; we had fun

We had seasons in the sun

But the wine and the song

Like the seasons have all gone

We had joy; we had fun

We had seasons in the sun

But the wine and the song

Like the seasons have all gone.

Seasons In The Sun

By Terry Jack

I would like to thank the following people for standing behind me and helping make this book a reality. Our journey in life introduces us to people who are inspiring angels; following are my angels. I wish to thank all the angels I may have forgotten to mention.

Lizzy McNett (book advisor, editor, production team)

David Allen Wolf (roommate and friend)

Dr. Shelley Stockwell (dear friend, mentor, educator, published author)

Kathi Botnen-Kenedi (friend, educator, mentor)

Pamela Kelly (friend, educator at UCLA, published author)

Lisa Allred-Lueken (friend, published author)

Ken Owens (friend, published author)

Richard Rumble (friend, educator, stage hypnotist)

Sandi G (entertainment agent)

Dr. Richard Neves (friend, educator)

Natalie Verdugo (friend, business entrepreneur)

David Almaraz (loving brother, father, husband)

Josie Almaraz (loving sister, mother, wife)

Mario Almaraz (loving brother)

Keith Dykes (friend, educator, entrepreneur)

Judy Umansky (friend, nurse, former Navy nurse)

Dona Lafaurie (friend, beautician, entrepreneur)

Jon Nicholas (friend, business manager, entrepreneur)

Roderic Dohleman (friend, computer tech, consultant)

R. Kevin Stevens (friend, manager, event coordinator)

Roy Robbins (friend, business owner, entrepreneur)

DR, TK Marie, TK Clinical Psychologist, Millennial Life Skill Coach (inspiration for this book)

Craig Duswalt (marketing coach, speaker)

ENDORSEMENTS

"As a therapist, Michael Almaraz has the ability to pinpoint a client's limiting belief structure and help empower those individuals to heal their old obstacles; thus, allowing them to reach new heights of both personal and professional success. In this book, he reminds us that our daily thoughts play a significant role in our behaviors and choices. Michael teaches us how to stay positive and productive while still being flexible to adjust to life's ever-changing situations."

Ken Owens, International Selling Author, ***Branding Your Character***

"Michael has taught me how to move forward in my life with self-respect; while enabling me to reach for my best self and live each day within a truly elevated path

of awareness. Through Michael's coaching, I was able to find my former loving-self and soar once again. I have learned to choose happiness and positivity! Thank you Michael, for all you have done for me and so many others. This book will allow many more people to be touched by your gift of healing. Your work is making a powerful change in the world."

Diane Spiegel, Community Fundraiser and Volunteer

"Michael is a mastermind trainer and has written a nifty handbook for your happiness, health, and success. Follow his advice and make your dreams come real!"

Shelley Stockwell-Nicholas, PhD

President of the International Hypnosis Federation

"Michael Almaraz's new book/workbook is _Abundantly You;_ it is full of useful tools to assist you in creating a balanced and abundant life. I recommend this book to any and all seekers."

Richard Neves, PhD

About Michael

Michael Almaraz is a motivational speaker and life coach in the areas of sales, personal and trans-personal development, and professional and corporate development.

He has over twenty years of private practice experience and currently operates two offices in Southern California.

Michael works with Olympians and Junior Olympians, helping them recognize their full potential in both sports and academics. He also finds that consulting with business owners from small to large corporations is a rewarding experience. Group training and private sessions have proven valuable to clients in terms of improving their business success.

Raised in a small town just outside Sedona, Arizona, Michael was drawn to the magic of influence and hypnosis. Being the youngest of five children, he quickly learned how to be heard. He understands the importance of being recognized. Both these skills are necessary to achieve success.

Michael suffered a devastating loss when his mother passed away in 1996. The transition left his emotions swirling in an uncontrollable spin. He found himself suffering from deep depression. The learned behaviors from his childhood created an emotional foundation, and his evolution toward recovery began. To treat the depression, Michael started using hypnosis and NLP. After two years, he had achieved success. With his great accomplishment, he trained and studied to obtain a double certification in the arts of hypnosis and NLP.

Michael has been active with the American Board of Clinical Hypnotherapy and the International Hypnosis Federation. He is currently a certified trainer and instructor, as well as an active board advisor for the International Hypnosis Federation. Michael has served on the Critical Incident Response Team (CIRT) for Delta Airlines. In addition, he has a certification in Transpersonal Hypnotherapy and Pain Management with Hypnosis. His sessions include hypnotherapy, neuro-linguistic programming and timeline therapy, as well as spiritual counseling.

His speaking programs include one-hour overviews, keynote addresses, full-day in-service seminars, and weekend to weeklong workshops.

Let Michael help you and your staff take the first step toward positive change, reaching your highest level of potential. Live a healthier and more productive life filled with happiness and joy for daily living.

To book Michael, please email him at

Michael@deeperstate.com

Michael Almaraz CHT, NLP, RP

www.deeperstate.com

info@deeperstate.com

How To Use Your New Toolbox/Workbook

Abundantly You was created to help you develop a more balanced and happier life.

Visit www.deeperstate.com/abundantlyyou to download the workbook. It is an additional guide that will help you explore a deeper state of yourself.

Abundantly You is based on one-day workshops called "Abundantly You." Most students believe that abundance is only financial in nature, and that they would lack love or spirituality. Sometimes they even deny themselves good health.

The human brain is a very complicated and misunderstood tool, with unlimited potential and learning opportunities. During my education as a clinical hypnotherapist and Neuro-Linguistic Programmer, I learned that our habits as humans (and animals) lead to specific outcomes. Our systems react to stimuli, either good or bad, and the result may be beneficial or a hindrance.

As an example: When people are stuck in a pattern stemming from negativity, the neurological system receives information that is either painful or pleasurable. Keep in mind that sometimes things that are bad can make you feel good, and that after an extended period, the pain can become a painful pleasure. Some individuals may survive in this rut for a lifetime. The mind makes changes using two powerful emotions: anger and pleasure. During these situations, lasting changes are created.

In clinical practice, giving unpleasant homework to a client will most likely not bring about change. Yet a pleasurable assignment will probably create positive results. Once I understood the learning curve of creating stimuli to alter the unconscious mind in a pleasurable way, I realized that change is possible with lasting success. The brain must feel good about the alteration; otherwise, it will ignore the suggestion.

The techniques in this book will bring about an accelerated change in your life and a deeper state of mind in all the ways you live. With all my blessings, move forward and create the all-powerful, balanced you!

Michael Almaraz CHT, NLP, RP

CHAPTER ONE:

State of Mind

How States of Mind Influence

When you create a mind state, remember to be clear about your intentions.

Created thoughts must be formulated with love and good energy, so they manifest positive outcomes. Remember, put out only what you're willing to accept in return; life brings forth what you desire and request. Optimistic ideas bring clear results. Negative intentions bring negative results. You receive what you request. A miserable person who constantly complains will bring down the emotions of those around them. Your brain can handle only so much negativity before overload overcomes oneself – followed by frustration and anger.

You generally move in the direction of a dominant thought to make a conscious decision. Multiply the good thoughts that direct your body to follow. If your brain believes something, your body will respond. Don't forget to create a winning attitude!

I like to have my clients imagine that they're in a "brain bar" and that they approach the bartender to order a "cocktail of anger!" The bartender will return with the peptides and neurons necessary to create this "anger cocktail."

Don't Become a Negaholic!

Now, if the client keeps ordering an anger cocktail, the bartender will move all the ingredients to the front because he/she knows what the client's next order is going to be. Just like an alcoholic, your brain will get drunk on it and crave it more and more. If you allow it to do so, it will become your emotion of choice.

Notes for a More Abundant You

CHAPTER TWO:

Robot Memory

Imagine your brain as a computer and your body as a robot. The drive tower (brain) controls the machine. Humans make decisions based on what their minds perceive as reality: decisions that we construct daily. If you believe that making money is easy and a positive aspiration because you haven't known otherwise, achieving wealth is much easier. The same applies to love and relationships – it will expel the energy to look for what it wants, not what it has already been through. Now, if your past was great and you're manifesting abundance, why change? Don't vary what's working ... just alter as needed!

Many years ago, I worked with a client who constantly said that her life was a "pile of crap." Everything she touched or attempted would "turn into crap!" Numerous times, we discussed how she was going to relive the past. I asked her what she realized from her experiences. She stated that it was "a pile of crap" and that she had learned nothing at all!

One day I responded to her: "You keep replaying the same old pile all the time. Is that right?"

She replied, "Yes!"

I said, "Let's see how we might alter your circumstances to change your emotions!"

The statement made her contemplate what needed to change, not what was staying the same. Participating in what was learned from the past and altering the memory toward a positive energy flow will change your life.

As a child, were you raised to believe in yourself, and can you achieve your goals if desired? If not, did your parents say, "Jim, life is a struggle, getting by is difficult"? Or possibly, "Carol, women aren't suited for that type of career!"?

On May 6, 1954, Robert Bannister ran a four-minute mile, which no one believed was physically possible! Today, running that distance isn't incomprehensible. If you trust yourself, you can accomplish your goals! This is hypnosis! (For more information about the four-minute mile, query Google or your search engine.)

Upgrade Your Robot:

Just because you were programmed one way doesn't mean you can't make modifications. They say it takes 30 days for the brain to accept something and become a routine, but I believe you can do it in an instant! One day is nothing when you have rest of your life. You must change your thoughts to new ones (such as, 'I AM worthy of a loving relationship,' or 'I AM worthy of a certain job that I enjoy and love').

Begin changing your memory and do an upgrade by thinking in abundance. When an outside influence gives you a negative emotion, convert it into a positive outcome. Use the undesirable situation to change the result. You don't have to suffer from your bad emotions unless you allow them to control your life. Remember, you aren't going to change the past! However, you have the ability to create a new future and the feelings that are connected to living fulfilled.

Remember: Extraordinary people
are ordinary individuals who think
and do extraordinary things!

To become a person who lives on this level, you should believe in spirituality and metaphysical laws. Your actions will cause a reaction. When you treat anyone with disrespect, the situation will break down and deteriorate. We are a charitable society in a taking world. We must pay it forward to receive what our hearts truly desire. However, we must do this with good intentions and faith. Seek out situations in which you can do good. It may be as simple as leaving a tip, helping friends and expecting nothing in return, or showing someone unconditional love and friendship (probably one of the hardest things to do). Give what you're willing to lose and relinquish!

We're going to review relationships and the emotional result.

Were you left in sorrow? How bad did this make you feel? Think about your mindset or emotions after an incident with a family member. The feelings didn't come from the person who hurt you. Your brain created them in this situation; the individual didn't cause your pain. I understand this concept may seem foreign, but you must decide ... either carry these sentiments with you, or let go and give them a positive change!

After the incident, who's in pain? You are, not the other person. Scan your hurts and learn from them. Take constructive thoughts into your next situation. Keep your mind neutral and encouraging. In life, you must be flexible and able to adjust to your situations. Most importantly, your emotions must be given directions. Regret is an opportunity for mental advancement. Grieve the loss and press on. Let the past empower you.

Let go of what isn't yours. **Get up, Get out, and Get going** ... learn and graduate to another level in life's journey.

Notes for a More Abundant You

CHAPTER THREE:

Create and Formulate Change

Visualize to create and change your situations. Manifest them as if they've already happened. For example: "I'll be driving a new Mercedes Benz SL class with a blue interior and white exterior by this time next year!" Give it a specific deadline and stay focused.

Once you're ready to visualize your thoughts, they must be clear and precise; be exact with your wants and desires. Focus the energy. Don't leave it scattered; this is called the power of intention. For example, a woman may say, "I need a date!" She'll venture out and look to meet guys. She'll find potential suitors, but her attempt is faulty. She didn't manifest her desires in detail (the more specific, the better). Everything – including our feelings – is energy. Feelings begin with an electrical charge in your neurons. When you expel bad vitality, it's like having a radio station that's not properly tuned. Your thoughts will give your brain different ideas.

I can tell you that, in my practice, this happens more often than you can imagine. I see clients who are looking for what they want, but aren't willing to focus on what they really desire. To formulate the changes and desires in your life, you must know what you want from the beginning. This is the only way to bring your goal manifestation to the next level. I find that it makes no difference whether the goal regards relationships, financial gains, or better health and peace. The important step is to stop talking about what you **don't** want and to start thinking about what you **do** want. However, keep in mind what is already working. It's very much like taking inventory of where you are and what tools you already have in your toolbox. You can then start putting out universal energy toward what you still need.

I find that many people spend a lot of time talking about how difficult something is, or how situations or people block them from success. Taking action is all about growth. You must formulate your change and live it. I always like to say that the actor going into a role, knowing he or she can become the part, will get the lead. However, this is only if the actor wants it passionately. You must be able to feel and know in your nervous system what success you desire. Live as if you already have the thing you want. Know what it looks like, feels like, sounds like, and even smells like.

In the past, I had a client who wanted to do better in life but didn't know how to achieve his dreams. He knew what he wanted, but he didn't know how to get there.

Our sessions worked on what he wanted. First, it helped that he understood this part of my therapy. He knew he wanted to own a shipping business. (He was tired of working as a dispatcher on the docks at the Port of Los Angeles.) After one of our sessions, he came out of a trance with the idea that he had to immerse himself into his new life. I asked him how he would do this.

In my office, I had a lemon that one of the other therapists had given me. My client picked up the lemon and asked if he could have it. We began discussing his plan. First, he would rent an office and ship the lemon with his first paid transport. However, this had to be done before the lemon went bad. It took about a month.

As I kept working with him, he told me he was going into his new office and laying on the floor, because there was only a desk and a phone. He would lay on the floor and use my self-hypnosis program to enter a dream-state. There, he would formulate what he needed for the next step of success. This young man ended up finding investors at his place of work. At the end of 30 days, he had his first truck. It has now been 10 years, and since then he has purchased 15 trucks. Plus, he added an international import and export business. Talk about formulation and moving the energy!

You see, there isn't a huge difference between the young lady looking for the love of her life and the client looking to start his own trucking business. You must have a plan, know what you want, and formulate your outcome as you need it to be.

Fear of the unknown is the only thing that will hold you back. Tell your mind the story of how you know it will be, and it shall become.

In closing, plan your future with great detail and specificity. Your thoughts and dreams can never be too small – think big! If you limit your visions, the outcomes will be stunted. What do you have to lose? Money isn't necessary to manifest happiness and wealth.

Notes for a More Abundant You

CHAPTER FOUR:

How to Mediate Your Outcomes

A creative visualization is a powerful tool. When you combine it with meditation and hypnosis, you become empowered. Is it possible to will something and make it happen? Yes, your belief in your probabilities of success and your emotional state will increase because you have laid the foundation for change. What you deem important prompts your thoughts and energy in that direction.

Children don't limit their wants. Did you eat, sleep, and dream of the prize? The visions became real, as if you already had the item to enjoy. As time passed, did you eventually obtain that thing? Young people create their outcomes because they believe without doubt, until the day comes when someone tells them differently.

Adolescents haven't been influenced by society, which alters our critical thought and unconscious. Kids are growing and maturing; they're discovering themselves. In this process, their wants, likes, and desires evolve, which enables them to envision and feel emotions. In essence, the visual cognizance runs wild. The result is the achievement of the dream.

To conquer the visualization, search your mind for a time when you were playing with your imaginary toy: a bike, pony, skateboard, etc. Think about how it made you feel. Now use the same passion to manifest your success and needs as an adult. Create a plan and grow the resources to make it happen. Anything is possible if you can visualize the outcome as reality.

How to Meditate and Manifest

Your meditation place must be quiet and free from distractions. You will need something to cause eye fixation, such as the flame of a candle. Alternatively, you can simply focus on a spot on the ceiling. If you're sitting in a car, look up at a large, puffy cloud.

Begin working on your breathing. As you fixate on your subject, take long, deep, full, and slow breaths. Imagine them becoming heavy and allow them to close. Now envision a large blackboard covering the wall. Visualize the number 99 at the top. Begin seeing the numbers melt, drip, drop, and float down as you regress. The falling digits bring about the relaxation. When you get to about 95, try opening your eyes. If you can't, you're in a trance state. Continue counting until your eyes won't open. The technique takes practice. If it doesn't work the first few times, don't give up; keep trying.

Once you're in the meditative state, begin formulating the manifestations of your desires. However, remember to stay realistic. Set an alarm for about 20-30 minutes in case you fall into REM sleep. Falling into a permanent trance and being unable to wake up is an old misconception. How many people have you seen stuck in a trance? Our relaxation MP3s will get you into meditation quicker and easier. You can order the products from our website @deeperstate.com.

Notes for a More Abundant You

CHAPTER FIVE:

Creating a Dream Chart

Create a Dream Chart, Not a Resolution

If you want to set a New Year's resolution, make an effort toward a worthwhile cause and try creating a dream chart. I'm sure you're thinking, 'What is a vision board?' Take pictures you like from magazines and paste them onto a poster board. Make sure the pictures relate to your goal and reflect what you want to happen in your life in the coming year. Look at each image; evoke the feelings captured by the reality of acquiring the items throughout the year. Keep this board in your office, a bedroom, or a place where you will see it every day. Trust in your ideas and manifest them into reality.

Many tools are available to help anyone who seeks any kind of resolution. However, I truly

believe that hypnosis is the best avenue. Tailored hypnosis audio programs allow for supervision and guidance as you walk through the process and create outcomes on all levels.

My relaxation MP3s are great tools for self-hypnosis and work very well for those who use them. You can order the MP3s @ deeperstate.com. We offer a workshop called "A Visionary Journey." Anyone is invited to join; allow me to help you move forward in creating the life you want and deserve. Please keep up to date with class schedules and tools designed to assist in the joy of personal empowerment.

Positive Confessions

In simple terms, confession is a declaration of belief. It is transforming your thoughts or ideas into words. The expressions are spoken aloud with positive undertones emphasized in pursuit of desired beneficial outcomes. Confidence is essential to achieve true inner peace. In some cases, certain obstacles require strong credence. Religious believers wouldn't be serving devoid of faith. The fastest human in the world wouldn't show up on the track without belief in their speed. Conviction alone brings about powerful benefits and solitude.

A man sitting in a coffee shop is occupied with thoughts that fall into his realm of thinking. An inventor wouldn't start a project if they didn't have the mental tools to accomplish the task. Words are sharper and much more potent than we give them credit for. A consistent declaration of a condition aligns your environment with your thoughts. Those liberties choose the state of mind and transform life, especially if they're negative. Learning positivity is important no matter what the circumstances; it's what you choose to believe. We can overcome any obstacle and become anything we desire. Remember, situations are temporary. The confessing act becomes a habit, and affirmative outcomes will be constant. Stay positive! Confess positively!

Acceptance of the person you are is critical. Walk the streets, be certain you're the best there is, get high on life! Inner peace is ground-breaking evidence of the possibilities you can achieve.

You'd agree that optimistic outcomes cannot stem from anger, resentment, and all other vices. The concept of fulfillment is nothing magical; it's simply a state of mind and a choice. If two people have similar lives, but one is happy while the other carries around hatred and bitterness, the results appear in small things like their clothing. One outfit will be clean and pressed, the other wrinkled and worn. The difference between these two is merely a decision; the choice is about neatness. The same applies to positive and negative individuals, the adoption of clear, precise actions.

Being factual is the acknowledgment of difficult times and choosing to remain positive. During those situations, you can build a constructive attitude. A young boy loses his mother and mourns her death; nonetheless, he is determined to become successful. He accepts the difficulty but chooses to deal with the loss and move forward.

Research surveys on regular gym attendance show that when a person hurts the most during a workout, he/she gets the best results. The deliberate decision at a painful moment is a decisive

action. The choice will launch you above
and beyond any circumstance in your life.

Notes for a More Abundant You

CHAPTER SIX:

Finding a Circle

The phrase, "Show me your friends and I'll tell you who you are," though completely true, is incomplete. It should say, "Show me your friends and I'll tell you who you will become." "When a tortoise lives too long with a lizard, it will increase its speed" implies that the lizard will influence the tortoise's speed. This phrase is erroneous! The lizard isn't making the tortoise faster. This may mean that you will need to align yourself with friends who support your new goals.

Change, in all its glory, is a function of choice. The alteration is the aftermath of choosing. Our certitudes are basic to the person inside.

The election to transform affects your decisions and, ultimately, you. Only those close to you know about your plans and can affect your paths before you travel them.

The second phrase states that your friends can make you a better person. They have the connection to augment a weakness into a strength. The choice must not be taken lightly. Surround yourself with individuals who have the same dreams and drive to motivate. However, be certain you seek out several others who have what you want.

To understand this example, colleagues on the same level raise your ambitions, while other colleagues drive you to surpass them. This is a win-win for you. Thus, the pursuit of people you want to emulate will push you past your limitations. I say, "Choose better."

I once met a group of college students at a restaurant. They seemed to be excited about something. After much fun, they gave their order and ate. It was time to settle the bill, but after divvying up the totals, one student didn't have enough to pay his portion. Instead of quibbling over the issue, everyone else chipped in and gladly paid for him. They maintained his dignity and boosted him to keep pushing. The moral here is that friends help each other. Always strive to become more than you are today; don't be afraid to pull the poison ivy from your garden of life.

Notes for a More Abundant You

66

CHAPTER SEVEN:

Love Yourself

Confidence is essential to succeed in life. It is the path upon which you walk into your dreams. There is one simple requirement and that is to love yourself. Ignore the faults or body parts you don't like. Simply march with assurance. If you trust something, you must first fancy it.

That is natural. Therefore, consign unconditional love to yourself.

Albert Einstein must have loved his brain. Surgeons love their hands because they do the amazing job of saving lives. When you give, you get love in return. The law of attraction states that what is given is received. There is nothing wrong with loving yourself. It takes only a small amount of real adoration to reap the rewards. By committing to yourself, success is imminent.

When doubt squashes the plan, the only one who is hurt – or who lives a life that is lacking

– is you. Look in the mirror and imagine how much talent you retain. It's enough to make you invincible. The person who loses through doubt or hurt is you. Except this no longer applies because you love yourself. Right?

When we say things like, "I hate myself for that," and get mad, we cannot love ourselves. Next time, change the words to create positive feedback and be confident. Know that

Love Yourself

you acted in everyone's best interest at the time. Be confident! Believe! Trust!

Smile often and appreciate yourself for a job well done rather than beating yourself up for mistakes. Others' impressions don't matter. They haven't walked in your shoes. They see only what you let them see, so you alone know everything about yourself. Don't keep your capabilities to yourself; own them and stand up. They're yours! Smile and tell the world about them.

Have you ever wondered about self-esteem, or how to get more of it? Do you think your self-esteem is low? Do you know how to tell? Do you know what to do?

Self-esteem answers the question, "How do I feel about who I am?" We learn self-esteem through childhood and living life. We don't inherit it.

Self-esteem is made up of the thoughts, feelings, and opinions we have about ourselves. Over time, habits of negative thinking about ourselves can diminish our value. Sometimes, people don't even realize they're negative thinkers!

Once you become aware of self-doubt, a change occurs in the way you think. When we change the way we feel about ourselves, we change the way we look at ourselves. The vision on the inside alters the images on the outside.

Focus on what goes well for you. Are you so used to focusing on your problems that they're all you see? Next time you catch yourself dwelling on problems or complaints about yourself or your day, find something positive with which to counter it. Write down three good things about yourself and three things that went well that day because of your efforts.

Notes for a More Abundant You

CHAPTER EIGHT:

It's All About Money

Every day, we are concerned about making money – the highest amount possible. Yet, we are continually told that money is evil. If too many bad things happen, prosperity changes everything. The information is correct; money won't make you happy, but in a way, it's like oxygen. Money is a necessary tool to survive in society. The key is to have the right amount. Everyone is different and requires unique balances.

I remember teaching a class on abundance. A young lady raised Catholic had been instructed to not seek material things in her life. The dilemma raised serious concerns. She wanted to buy a mid-level sports car, but the purchase created feelings of guilt about paying for such an extravagance.

Our conversation started, and I asked, *"So, you work for a nonprofit raising money to help fight laws that go against people who have no one and who lack money to defend themselves. Is that correct?"*

She answered, *"Yes, my chosen career. But there have been many times when my car has given me troubles, and I'm unable to reach some of my clients."*

The advice was a no-brainer. I said, *"Imagine if we went beyond buying a reliable car that would get you to your appointments on time. How many more people would you be able to help? Let's look at this situation another way; if you double your income, how much more could you do to give back?"* She left my class self-assured and comfortable with her decision to purchase the car.

The ability to attract money involves a rigorously honest self-appraisal of exactly where you are financially. When you have acquired this knowledge, you can start to build. This is unlike the reality or fantasy of someone who refuses to accept their situation.

The next stage involves making creative use of the subconscious to raise your self-belief. This can give you inspired ideas for creating money. Your subconscious does, indeed, have all the answers and is the most effective wealth building tool. Therefore, to manifest goals to earn money, you must begin to use it – through hypnosis.

The abilities to develop financial freedom, gain the desire to make money through self-hypnosis, and understand the laws of prosperity aren't impossible or even difficult to acquire. Success in creating wealth lies within a person's mental attitude, and by extending their psychological frame of mind. Attracting abundance and creating wealth requires a strong desire for independence. You must believe in the concept.

The conscious mind develops thoughts based on what you do or don't believe. Your subconscious guides you toward – and attracts – conditions and events, represented by the nature of your conscious thought. In other words, if you habitually think of abundance and success, your subconscious will guide you and attract wealth and prosperity. If you usually think of scarcity, your subconscious will guide you toward – and attract – scarcity, hardship, and poverty.

Negative perceptions and beliefs about money and wealth are rooted in the scarcity mindset. You become blind to reality and, more specifically, sightless to the knowledge of how to manifest money. The ability to create wealth already exists in the subconscious. It is a matter of fine-tuning your mind to notice the opportunities for wealth creation swirling around you every day – even in challenging financial times. So, bear in mind that success in manifesting prosperity is based primarily on your attitude toward economic freedom. If you're continuously stressed about poverty, you're pushing away success. Learn to develop a relaxed, open, conscious frame of mind toward wealth creation and success. Worrying about your perceived lack will get you nowhere. Self-hypnosis is an ideal and efficient method of training your conscious mind to discard negative deliberations, and to replace them with decisive considerations. These new deliberations will enable you to fulfill your potential, and to acquire the wealth and financial security you want and deserve. Many people don't have enough money because of their mental attitudes. Luck has nothing to do with it.

The reality isn't an oversimplification. Financial opportunities surround us, regardless of the "state of the economy." However, to intuitively spot the instances and confidently use them, we must develop a prosperity consciousness.

Most people – to varying degrees – have a scarcity consciousness. The conscious thoughts are dominated by what appear to be the reasons for a lack of money and the barriers preventing them from generating wealth:

> ➤ "I don't have the know-how."
> ➤ "I don't have the resources."
> ➤ "I don't have the contacts."
> ➤ "I don't have the funds to start with."
> ➤ "I have too much debt, etc. etc."

By the end of the day, with all these negative notions, they aren't one cent richer.

By consciously and habitually thinking along these lines, they're ensuring that the ability to make money and gain financial freedom remains as far out of their reach as possible. The all-powerful subconscious mind works tirelessly to reveal your life and whatever thoughts or images your conscious thought habitually impresses upon it. The obvious lesson to be learned about money – and anything else – is that focusing on the negative is counterproductive.

The tendency to focus on the negative reasons why something can't be accomplished originates from deep-rooted negative self-beliefs. They can be subtle, but they are very powerful and will indeed keep you in financial destitution for the rest of your life – if you allow them to do so.

In Summary

"A Visionary Journey" student recently informed me that she had made her decision: a new Tesla. Her work production had doubled, with the bonus of saving the earth. I'm proud of her actions and changes.

Negative self-beliefs help sustain the scarcity mentality and act as mental blocks – barriers existing only in the mind, but that busily provide emotional, or even seemingly rational, reasons why you should not or could not achieve wealth and financial security.

Notes for a More Abundant You

CHAPTER NINE:

Don't Be in a Hurry

Life zooms by at the speed of light, with slow phases in between, so pause and take a moment to enjoy living. Teaching is a rigorous process, but only half as much as learning. It takes time to heal. It also takes time to learn. New skin slowly covers a wound, protecting the body from further damage. Emotional wounds heal in the same way. We learn, and the pain becomes part of us. The process is best described as gradual, progressive, and in steps. The brain can hold only so much new information each day, which grows with your experience. When someone sets their goals too high, the brain shuts down, creating anxiety and disappointment. We make it almost impossible to be happy with our plans.

My freshman year of high school was the first time I was exposed to diverse people in large numbers. I mingled and met a very beautiful and studious young lady. She hardly spoke, but we got along. Over time, her mannerisms became predictable.

She was a solemn person. Being a curious cat, I studied her for some time before I finally asked, "Joan, why don't you smile?"

Her reply: *"If that's all it took to get good grades, I would smile."*

The statement was shocking, but with some help she started smiling more. The explanation was that her goals consumed her attention, so her studies required learning everything in each course daily. The burden weighed heavily on her mind. The stress brought on sadness and gnawed at her insides. Many people are in similar situations. Give yourself a break!

It's imperative to consistently stop and look at the progress you've made. Revel in achievements and shout them out to the world! It's gradual, not overnight, so take your time, smile, and get it right.

Notes for a More Abundant You

CHAPTER TEN:

Author's Poem

Focus

I wandered around the world

Looking for a suitable place for my

world

I mingled and giggled

I struggled to reach the rich of life's

cycle

I joined every vehicle
But found myself roaming a circle

Then my soul awakens
And whispers I am undefined

Diverted is the mind that flies about
Having no target in mind
Divided is the heart
That lacks concentrating act
'Cuz there lies attraction that causes
distractions
He who lacks destination in sight
Feels every situation right

But one way leads to the top
The ladder of focus
With strong built steps
Of persistence

Consistency

Less tense

And absence of pretense

These steps, though tough, lead to the

top

Never give up, let up, or shut up

Till you have reached up, stored up, paid

up

and stayed up

Then, you have your ability and

capability

Endowed by the divinity

Manifesting in reality

Get focused! Get fulfilled.

Write Your Own Poem

AUTHOR'S NOTE

Diversity is the basic measure of life. To a doctor, life is breathing, while to a nutritionist, it is healthy living. The professor might speak of education, while an athlete would focus on competition. My advice to you: Live life.

The choice of living depends on the person, whether it's higher grades, being a better person, giving more, or simply finding security within. It's all up to you! The <u>Abundantly You Workbook</u> can be regarded as active advice for when you need help being happier. If you're searching for positive affirmations or whatever the situation dictates, the message in this book is there to help you progress in life.

The Suggestions Guide takes you through step-by-step outlines to find the answers you seek. Everyone should make an effort to become a better person. Repetition over time will build what's called "muscle memory." Retention of this type is described as "part of you," and you become what you practice. Your confessions, reactions, and entire demeanor experience a fresh feel of happiness, and you'll have the emotional stability for new possibilities. You won't be bound to bad feelings of resentment for another. You won't be that negative person who, because of disappointment, finds fault with everything. More importantly, you'll be ready to take on anything, at any time.

As the saying goes: "Favor is when opportunity meets preparedness." You would be favored because opportunities come. Because you've changed, your mind will be prepared.

Lastly, you should know that a person who stands for nothing will fall for everything. This statement means that a person will know what they are and whom they want to become. They aren't mesmerized by whatever enters their space. Your stance is tethered to your belief and actions. Embedded in this workbook are the real-life steps to practice throughout life.

MORE WILL BE COMING. Live in love and balance!

Michael Almaraz, CHT, NLP, RP

BIBLIOGRAPHY

Brian Leslie Weiss (born November 6, 1944) is an American psychiatrist, hypnotherapist, and author who specializes in past life regression. His research includes reincarnation, past life regression, future life progression, and survival of the human soul after death

Betty Eadie. (born 1942) is a prominent American author of several books on near-death experiences (NDEs). Her best-known book is the No. 1 New York Times best-seller *Embraced by the*

Light (1992), describing her near-death experience.

Dale Carnegie (born November 24, 1888) was a pioneer in corporate training programs and the developer of famous courses in self-improvement, public speaking, and interpersonal skills. He was born Dale Breckenridge Carnagey in Maryville, Missouri.

Richard Bandler (born February 24, 1950) is a contemporary psychologist and self-help author who works primarily in the field of Neuro-Linguistic Programming (NLP). He studied psychology and philosophy at the University of California and earned his bachelor's degree in 1973.

Anthony J. Robbins (born February 29, 1960) is the author of several best-selling self-help books, including *Unlimited Power* and *Awaken the Giant Within*. Robbins has become something of a celebrity for his much-publicized "firewalk" seminars.

Robert B. Dilts has been a developer, author, trainer, and consultant in the field of Neuro-Linguistic Programming (NLP) – a model of human behavior, learning, and communication – since its creation in 1975 by John Grinder and Richard Bandler.